Revenge of the Goldfish

Upbeat, fun poems
for 4 - 7 year olds.

A.F. B. Griffey .. R. W. B. .. V. A. Webb

Illustrations: R. W. B. and TOMB

Louannvee Publishing

Copyright © A. F. B. Griffey 2016
Fire Engine, Lorry Driver copyright © R. W. B. 2016
Autumn Leaves, Don't copyright © V. A. Webb 2016
Illustrations copyright © R. W. B. & TOMB 2016

Moral rights asserted.

All rights reserved. No part of this publication may be reproduced, stored in a retrieval system, or transmitted, in any form or by any means electronic, mechanical, photocopying, recording or otherwise, without the prior written permission of the publisher.

ISBN 978-0-9935564-0-1

Published in the UK by:

Louannvee Publishing

www.louannveepublishing.co.uk

DEDICATION
To mums, dads, grannies, granddads and Auntie Ida.

This book belongs to:

_____

_____

Contents

— A. F. B. Griffey —

	Page
No Elves or Fairies in this Book	5
If I Could be a Giraffe	6
Blowing Bubbles at the Sun	7
The Washing Machine	8
A Dinosaur Ate my Teacher	9
Verity the Venomous Viper	10 - 11
Webcam	12
Zap!	13
My Wheelchair Zooms by 'Really Fast'	14 - 15
Revenge of the Goldfish	16 - 17
Spider in the Sandpit	18 - 19
Mobile Phone	24 - 25
Pink, Pink Bus	26
Real Live Robot	27
My Glasses	28 - 29
Revenge of the Rubbish	30 - 32

— R. W. B. —

	Page
Fire Engine	20
Lorry Driver	21

— V. A. Webb —

	Page
Don't	22
Autumn Leaves	23

No Elves or Fairies in this Book

There are no elves or fairies in this book.

Just turn the pages, take a look!

You will find ....

dinosaurs, robots too

and everyday things we often do

You will find....

computers and mobile phones.

You will find....

humans and human moans,

but....

no cutie cute fairies doing a dance.

No evil elves about to prance

because....

there are no elves or fairies in this book.

Just turn the pages, take a look!

A. F. B. Griffey

If I Could be a Giraffe

If I could be a giraffe, it would make me laugh

and

make me want to try...

to reach up tall, over the garden wall

and

munch big clouds from the sky.

Blowing Bubbles at the Sun

If I could be a bird,

it would be absurd.

I would soar to the clouds

for some fun.

I would sit right there,

in my favourite chair,

blowing big, soapy bubbles

at the sun.

The Washing Machine

The washing machine fell apart, in my hand.

Now there's water all over the floor.

The washing machine fell apart, in my hand.

I only just opened the door.

Now there's clothing piled high, right up to the sky and knickers and tights on the sink.

Now there's clothing piled high, right up to the sky and my socks, they're beginning to stink.

A Dinosaur Ate my Teacher!

"Miss Jones, Miss Jones.

There's a dinosaur, in the corridor

and it's really, really fierce.

        Miss Jones, Miss Jones

        Can't you see, it's looking at me?

        Its teeth look fit to pierce.

                Stop waffling on.

                We must be gone.

                We can't put up a fight.

It's coming in here.

I'm filled with fear.

What are we going to do?

Miss Jones,

Miss Jones.

That **dinosaur**

    from the corridor,

               is in here eating you!"

Verity the Venomous Viper

Look out!

It's Verity the venomous viper

going absolutely hyper.

    Escaped from her glass vivarium.

    Heading past the fish aquarium

    and through the herb herbarium.

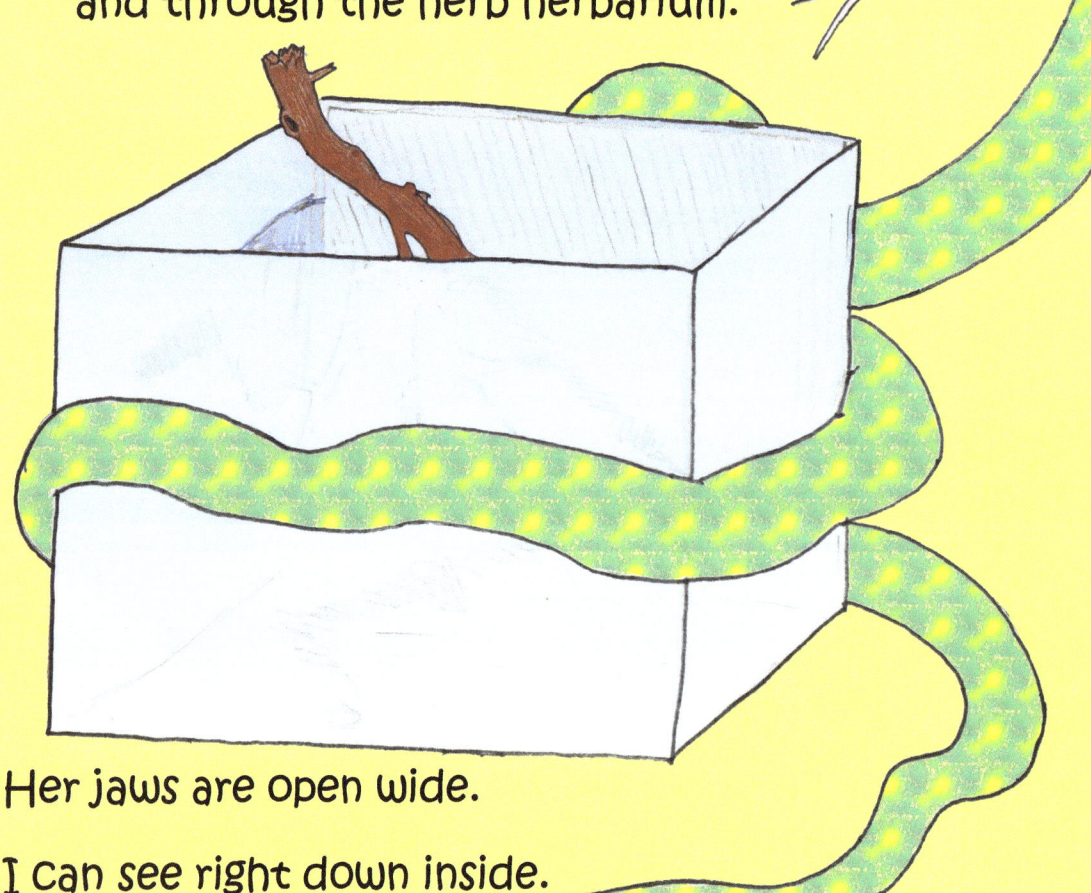

Her jaws are open wide.

I can see right down inside.

    Fangs forward for attack.

        You'll make a tasty snack!

Let me help you quick!

I'll distract her with a stick.

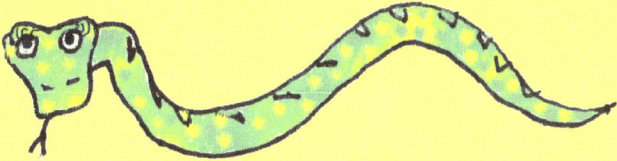

Wow! I've flicked her through the herbarium,

right over the fish aquarium,

back into her glass vivarium.

Cool!

Excellent! She's locked in safe and sound.

Now just her mate Vincent to be found!

Webcam

Shall we webcam Mars?

Are there aliens there?

        Can we webcam Mars?

        What would an alien wear?

Shall we contact another universe –

far, far away?

        Can we contact another universe –

        or would it take all day?

A. F. B. Griffey

I made our laptop screen look neat.

        I clicked the word that said **delete**,

zapped out files and pictures too

        and made that screen look clean and new.

I told my brother what I'd done.

        He yelled at me. I had to run......

My Wheelchair Zooms by Really Fast

"My wheelchair zooms by really fast.
Come on quick or you'll be last.

Come on! Quick -
let's have some fun!
Come on! Quick -
just run, run, run!

Oh... are you running out of puff?
Have you really raced enough?

Well jump up quick and hitch a ride.
Hold on tight now. Don't you slide.

Let's take this snaky path right here.
Look, I'll show you how to steer.
Come on quick! Mind that bush!
Through that puddle. Splash and swoosh!

Oh... are you looking
grey and groggy,
caked in mud and
very soggy?

Well jump down quick. Don't sit and ride.
I'll go real slow. You walk beside."

Revenge of the Goldfish

"Well.....

Enough is enough in the life of a fish.

I'd rather be roasted

and served on a dish,

than blow bubbles at glass, in your dreadful room

with a feeling of loneliness and ghastly gloom.

I think, you think my brain is small.

I think, you think I can't recall,

the things I've seen, whilst in your room,

swimming around in ghastly gloom.   But.....

I saw you chew chocolate — in the middle of the night.

I saw you dress as a ghost

and give your brother a fright.

I saw you pick your nose

and eat it with glee.

I saw you stick chewing gum

on your baby brother's knee.   So....

Watch out!

I'm preparing to escape.

I'm coming for you right now!

I'm coming to cause some trouble.

I'm coming to cause a row! I'm telling everyone about chocolate and other things I've seen.

I'm going to talk about chewing gum and noses.

Can't you see I'm really MEAN?

Oh.........

Is it suddenly feeding time?

Are you coming to say hello?

Well.........

Maybe I'll stay in my bowl a while.

It's not so bad you know!"

Spider in the Sandpit

There's a spider in the sandpit

and it's playing in the sand.

I know it's in there somewhere,

because I felt it on my hand.

I'm not really scared of spiders,

but I'm going back inside -

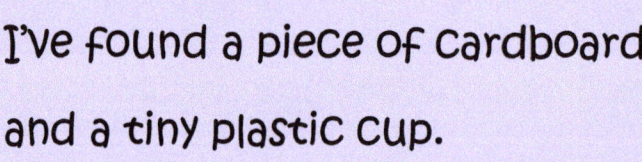

in case I squish the spider

and I hurt its spider pride.   Wait.....

I've found a piece of cardboard

and a tiny plastic cup.

Will the spider go on the cardboard?

Can I scoop it up?

Wow!

I'm guiding the spider gently,
towards the cup, with the card.
The spider's scuttling madly,
finding the journey really hard.

Excellent!

I've scooped the spider up.
The spider's safe and sound.

Look.....

It's squirming and wriggling happily
and running along the ground.

Cool!

Now I can play back in the sandpit
and make patterns in the sand,
because the spider's no longer in there
and it won't go on my hand.

Fire Engine! Fire Engine!

Fire engine! Fire engine! Please come quick!
Now the smoke's getting rather thick!
Fire engine! Fire engine! Roll out the hose.
Now that smoke's getting up my nose!
Fire engine! Fire engine! Water all about.
Hear the chief order and........................... shout!
Fire engine! Fire engine! Now the smoke has cleared
and the fire has disappeared!

Lorry Driver

I'm a lorry driver, driving down the road.

I'm a lorry driver, look at this heavy load.

Bumpy, bumpy, bumpy, bumpy, bumpy, bumpy, road.

I'm a lorry driver, driving down the road.

Don't

Don't
        run down
                the stairs
                        too fast.

You could land in such a heap.

You might kick the cat.

      He wouldn't like that

         and the spider is trying to sleep.

Shhhhh! It's spider siesta.

V. A. Webb

Mobile Phone

I have a special mobile phone,

all of my very, very own.

I ring and ring and talk all day.

I just don't want to go and play.

I press each button. Each makes a sound.

                     I call a friend to come around.

My friend's in the sandpit, over there.

Yes, over near that bright red chair.

"Not now" he says "I'm in the sand,

making tunnels with my hand."

So I press each button. Each makes a sound.

                     I call a friend to come around.

My friend's by the play dough over there.

Yes, really near that bright red chair.

"Not now" she says "Can't you see

I'm squishing snakes to eat for tea."

So I press each button, each makes a sound.

I call a friend to come around.

My friend's by the finger paints, over there.

Yes, really near that bright red chair.

"Not now" she says "I'm having fun,

making pictures for everyone."

So I press each button, each makes a sound. Then I tell my friends I'm coming round!

Oh—by the way.....

It's not really real, it's a toy you know.

It's on the red chair. You have a go.

Pink, Pink Bus

It's a pink, pink bus.

It's a pink, pink bus.

It's really, really cool.

It's a pink, pink bus.

It's a pink, pink bus,

taking us to school.

There are rainbow colours all inside and music playing as we ride.

It's a pink, pink bus.

It's a pink, pink bus.

It's really, really cool.

What happens, to the beat of the poem, if you say 'a yellow bus' or 'an indigo bus' instead of 'pink'? Why?

It's a pink, pink bus,

It's a pink, pink bus,

taking us to school.

Real Live Robot

I want a real live robot, with the power of a wild typhoon,

to share my days, to learn my ways and…..

beam me to the moon.

It must be made of metal, with huge great shiny feet.

No heavy heels.

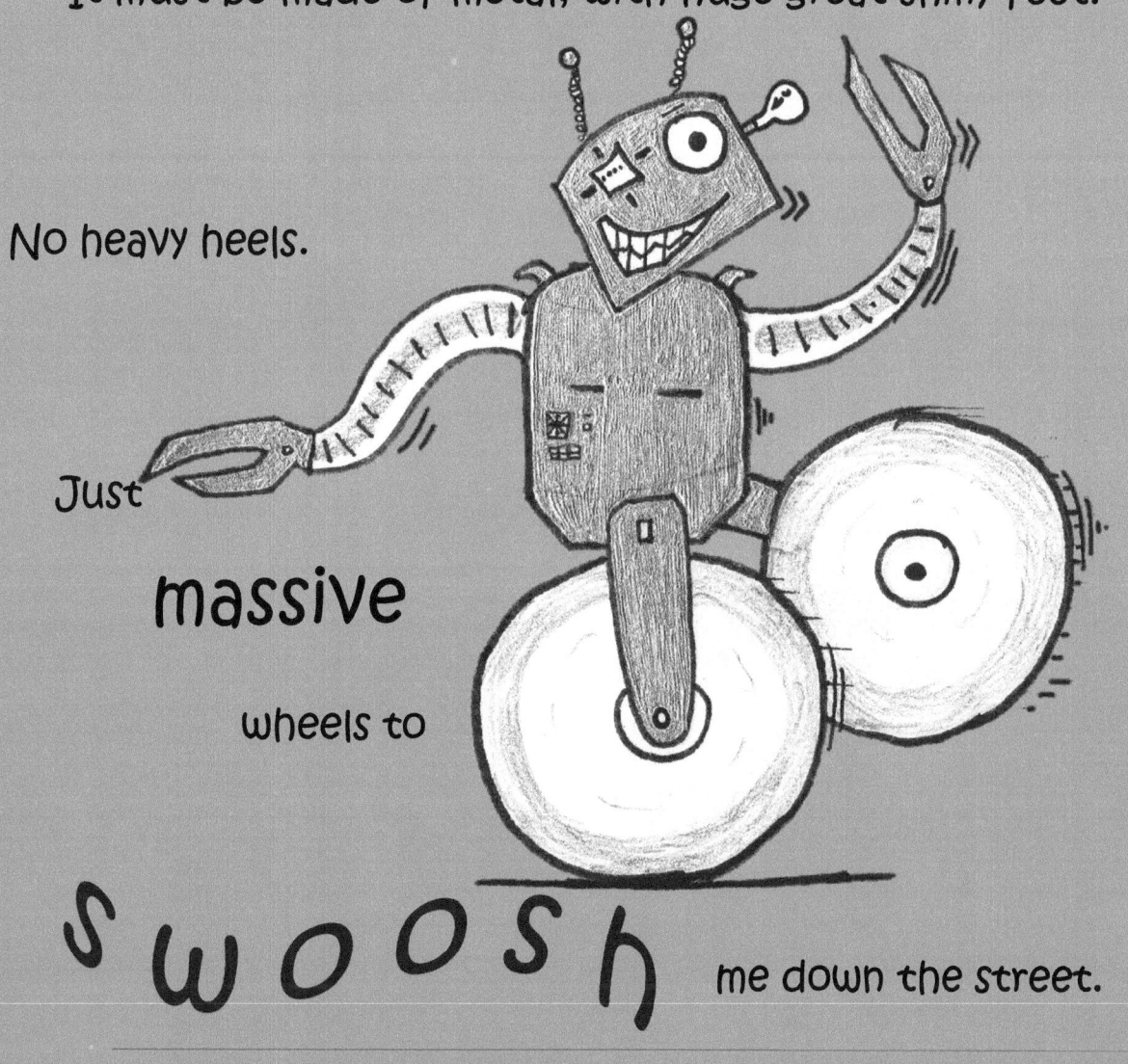

Just

massive

wheels to

swoosh

me down the street.

A. F. B. Griffey

My Glasses

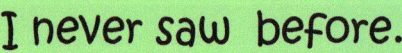

My glasses make me see things

I never saw before.

I don't fall down

the garden steps

or walk into the door.

I can find the missing piece of railway,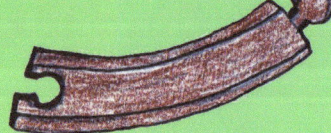

from my wooden railway track

and see my favourite t-shirt,

upon my clothing rack.

I don't sit on the baby
and make him give a wail.

I walk right round my kitten,
without treading on her tail.

I can even see a spider,
lurking in the hall
and my finger painting finger prints,
going up the wall,

but now that I can see things,
I never saw before,
I'm told to tidy all my toys up -
not leave them on the floor!

Revenge of the Rubbish

Soggy tissues,

chewed chewing gum,

leaky can of lemonade.

 Stinky socks,

slimy seaweed,

gluey model still unmade.

 Still they live within my room,

in that space behind my door.

Silently they merge and grow,

as they lie upon my floor.

Football boots,

 half eaten yoghurt,

piece of toast complete with mould.

 Squashed fly,

melted Ice cream,

toe nail clippings—really old.

Still they live, within my room,

in that space behind my door.

Silently they merge and gr**OW**,

as they churn upon my floor......

Continued.... quickly turn the page.... carefully!

Silently they rise to greet me,
swirl and whirl and try to eat me,
as I open up my door.
Slinking, stinking, oh so near me..,
Spinning, winning, they can HEAR ME,
as I yell behind my door....

"Mum....Dad....anyone, anywhere! Come and help me clean my floor!"

32

www.ingramcontent.com/pod-product-compliance
Lightning Source LLC
Chambersburg PA
CBHW041128300426
44113CB00003B/96